THE PHENOMENON OF THE SOUL

("VOICE OF INAYAT" SERIES)

BY

SHERIFA LUCY GOODENOUGH

SUFISM IS THE RELIGIOUS PHILOSOPHY OF LOVE
HARMONY AND BEAUTY

LONDON
THE SUFI PUBLISHING SOCIETY, Ltd.
86, Ladbroke Road, W.
1919

Kessinger Publishing's Rare Reprints
Thousands of Scarce and Hard-to-Find Books!

· · ·
· · ·
· · ·
· · ·
· · ·
· · ·
· · ·
· · ·
· · ·
· · ·
· · ·
· · ·
· · ·
· · ·
· · ·
· · ·
· · ·
· · ·
· · ·

We kindly invite you to view our extensive catalog list at:
http://www.kessinger.net

INAYAT KHAN

PREFACE

———

WHILE under the spiritual guidance of Pir-o-Murshid Inayat Khan, the bearer of the Sufi Message to the Western World, it has been my great privilege to hear from his voice things of the essential truth taught by all the great teachers of the world. Recognizing the value of his lectures, and considering of how great importance they would be during this time of the world's spiritual reawakening, I have tried to put on paper a record of them, and I have named it the "Voice of Inayat Series," with the hope that they will be helpful to those who tread this path.

SHERIFA LUCY GOODENOUGH.

April 3rd, 1919.

THE PHENOMENON OF THE SOUL

THE PHILOSOPHY OF THE SOUL

The soul is called in Sanskrit Atma, in Persian it is called Ruh. When the Prophet was asked, " What is the soul?" he answered in two words, " Umri Allah," " an activity of God."

The connection between the Consciousness and the soul is like the connection between the sun and the ray. The ray is formed by the activity of the sun shooting forth its light. The activity of the Consciousness shoots forth its ray, which is called the soul. Activity in a certain part of the Consciousness makes that part project itself toward the manifestation. The ray is the sun, but we distinguish the ray as apart, distinct with itself, longer or shorter, stronger or fading away, according to the state of activity in it.

The soul during its life on earth and after does not change its plane of existence; if any change takes place it is in the direction of its movement. The soul has originally no weight, but on its way

7

it gathers around it properties produced from itself, and borrowed continually from the elements which compose the universe, and as our possessions are not necessarily ourselves, so the properties are not the soul. The best comparison is with our eyes, in which vast tracts of country, huge mountains and miles of horizon on the sea are reflected at one time, and yet the eyes are scarcely an inch in length and width. Such is the nature of the soul, which is so small as to be counted one among the numberless souls contained in the universe and yet so vast as to contain within itself the whole universe.

The external self, the mind and the body, have confined a portion of the whole Consciousness; the same portion is in reality the soul. It is as if a line were drawn upon a cloth marking off a part of it as separate from the whole. Or it is as if we were to stand before a curtain with a small lantern so that the light of the lantern falls upon the curtain and forms a patch upon it. In like manner the impressions of the mind and body are reflected on the soul and separate it from the whole Consciousness. Upon the soul is reflected the happiness or misery, the joy or sorrow of the external self, but the soul in itself is neither sad nor joyful. The soul is neither subject to birth and death nor has it increase or decrease; it neither evolves nor degenerates.

If you stand before a mirror clothed in rags the mirror holds the reflection of your rags, but it is not itself in misery. If you stand before the mirror covered with pearls and diamonds the reflection of your pearls and diamonds falls upon the mirror, but the mirror does not turn into diamonds or pearls. So it is with the soul; neither is it a sinner nor is it virtuous; neither is it rich nor is it poor. All life's joy and sorrow, rise and fall, are reflected for the time being upon the curtain of the soul, and after a time pass away. It is therefore that both the joy and sorrow of yesterday are nothing to us to-day.

The soul and the body are the same essence, the soul has formed the body from itself, the soul being finer, the body grosser. What in the soul may be called vibration in the body becomes atom. The soul has become mind in order to experience more, it has become body in order to experience still more concretely; yet the mind is independent of the body, and the soul is independent of both mind and body.

The soul sees through the mind and the body, the body is the spectacles of the mind, and the mind is the telescope of the soul. It is the soul that sees, but we attribute sight and hearing to the eyes and ears. In absence of the soul neither the body nor the mind can see. When a person is dead the eyes are there, but they cannot see, the ears are there, but they cannot hear.

It is the work of the soul to know and to see, and it is the work of the mind and body to act as a magnifying glass for it. Yet they in their turn also see and hear what is external to them, as the Consciousness works through them also. The soul sees the play of thought in the mind, the mind perceives the pains and sensations of the body, the body is conscious of heat, cold and touch. Its consciousness may be seen when something is accidentally about to fall on it. Before the mind can think of a plan for safety the exposed part of the body instantly contrives its escape.

The mind sees the body alone, but the soul sees both the mind and the body; neither the body nor the mind is able to see the soul. The soul is accustomed to see what is before it, and so it cannot see itself. Our soul has always looked outward, that is why our eyes, nose, ears, all our organs of perception are outward. It is our mind and our body that attract our soul outward. And as the eyes, which see all things, yet need a mirror to see themselves, so the soul cannot see itself without a mirror.

When the eyes are closed, do you think that the soul sees nothing? It sees. When the ears are closed, do you think that the soul hears nothing? It hears. This proves that it is the soul that sees and hears. In the meditative life, by viewing the Anvar and Ansar, a Sufi realizes this fact, that there are objects which, without the help of the eyes, the soul can see, and there are sounds which, without the help of the ears, it can hear. The great poet Kabir has said: " What a play it is that the blind reads the Koran, the deaf hears the Gita, the handless is industrious, the footless is dancing." He refers to the soul which has the capacity of working even without instruments, such as the organs of the body and the faculties of the mind.

Sleep, the unconscious condition, is the original state of life, from which all has come. " The world was created out of darkness." Koran. As the body sleeps and the mind sleeps so the soul sleeps. The soul does not always sleep at the same time as the mind and the body. This sleep of the soul is experienced only by the mystics; they are conscious of this experience in themselves, and so can recognize it in others. The body sleeps more than the mind, the soul sleeps much less than either the mind or the body. When a person is fast asleep his soul does not lose its contact with the body. If the soul lost its contact with the body, the person would die; if the soul withdrew from the mind, the mind would be dispersed, the collection of thought would be scattered, it would be like a volcanic eruption.

The soul takes pleasure in the experience of the senses, in eating and drinking, in every experience. It indulges in this, and the more it indulges in it the more it becomes bound to this. All that we eat and drink contains a narcotic, even pure water. Therefore after eating and drinking a sort of sleep comes upon us, the soul feels a little relieved, it feels rather detached from the body. The soul cannot easily be free from the body and the mind. Though its real joy is to attain peace by being free from experience, yet it has forgotten this. " Happy is he who keeps it pure and lost is he who corrupts it." Koran. There are people who take strong drink, hashish, opium, drugs and all such things. Under their influence the troubles of the body are less felt and the thoughts are blurred, the soul feels relieved; but it is a transitory happiness because it is dependent upon matter instead of upon spirit.

The ordinary person knows that after deep sleep he is calm, he feels reposed, his feeling is better, his thoughts clearer. The condition of Hal or

Samadhi, the highest condition, is the same as that of deep sleep, the difference being only this that it is experienced at will. The difference between the perfect person and the ordinary person is only this, that the perfect person experiences consciously what the imperfect person experiences unconsciously. Nature provides all with the same experience, but most people are unconscious of the experience, which is to their disadvantage.

When the mind is dispersed no impression will remain on the soul, nothing will retain it from merging into the whole Consciousness.

It has been said by some philosophers that we are parts of God. That is not so. They have said this because they have seen the physical body. What more can the intellect see? In the physical existence, each individual is distinct and separate, but behind this physical existence all are one, the Consciousness is one. If it were not so we should not be able to know one another, neither the face nor the voice nor the language each of the other. We can know, if we advance spiritually, how our friend is; if he is in Japan or in Arabia and we are here, we can know if he is ill, whether he is sad or happy; and not the state of our friends only but everything is known to the advanced soul.

MANIFESTATION.

In the beginning, when there was no earth nor Heaven, there was no other phase of existence than the Eternal Consciousness, which in other words may be called a silent, inactive state of life or unawakened intelligence that man has idealized as God, the Only Being.

In the first stage of manifestation the unconscious state of existence turns into 'Ilm, Consciousness. Every soul is a ray of the Consciousness. The nature of the Consciousness is that it is radiant, it sends out rays. These pass through all the planes until they reach the ideal manifestation in man.

In the Vedanta the soul is called by three names which denote its three aspects, Atma, Mahatma, Parmatma. Atma is the soul conscious of the life on the surface, Mahatma is the soul conscious of the life within as well, Parmatma is the Consciousness that is the soul of souls, conscious of the absolute within and without, the God of the knower, the Lord of the seer.

In the primal stage of manifestation the Consciousness has no knowledge of anything save of being, not knowing in what or as what it lives. The next aspect of the Consciousness is the opposite pole of its experience, where it knows all that it sees and perceives through the vehicles of the lower world but is limited to this. When it rises above this experience and experiences the higher world as far as the highest aspect of its being, as said above, it becomes Mahatma, the Holy Ghost that unites Parmatma, the Father, with Atma, the Son, as explained in the terms of Christianity.

All this manifestation is constituted of two aspects of the Consciousness, power and intelligence, in poetical terms love and light. All power lies in the unintelligent aspect of the Consciousness, and the wisdom of the Creator that we see in the creation is the phenomenon of the intelligent aspect of the Consciousness.

All this creation is not created of anything that is outside of the Consciousness. It is the Consciousness itself which has involved a part of itself in its creation while a part remains as Creator, as water frozen turns into ice and yet water abides within and the ice lasts only for the time that it is frozen; when light reaches the ice it turns into water, its original element. So it is with the Consciousness; all things have been created out of it, and when their time of existence is finished all return and merge into it.

The Consciousness has taken four distinct steps in manifestation, which in the Sufic terms are called 'Ilm, 'Ishq, Ujud, Shuhud. 'Ilm is the stage in which the Consciousness acts as intelligence. 'Ishq is the stage when the activity of the rays of the Consciousness has increased and this has caused confusion among the rays and made power out of the intelligence, which is will in a simple term and in a poetical term love. The third step of the Consciousness is the creation of vehicles, such as mind and body, through which it experiences the life on the surface. And its fourth step is its conscious experience of life from the depth to its utmost height, which is called Shuhud, and this fulfils the purpose of all manifestation.

The divisions of one into many are caused by light and shade, and if we looked keenly into life, both within and without, we should realize clearly that it is one life, one light, which appears divided and made into many by different shades. Every luminous object under the shadow of a less luminous object turns darker in part, and this in the term of art is called shade. It is this secret which is hidden under the variety of things and beings.

Time and space are the cause of all creation and the source of all its variety. It is time that changes things and beings from the raw state to the ripe condition, from youth to age, from birth to death. Time brings rise and fall, and space gives success and failure. A person may meet with failure in one place and in another place with success, in one country he may rise and in another country he may fall. If one were to look closely into life one would see that all creation is changed under the influence of time and space whereas no change ever takes place in space or in time. It is in these that the mystery of the whole world abides.

The activity of the Consciousness has two aspects, motion and stillness, which cause two distinct things, the expressive power and the faculty of response. From the highest to the lowest plane of existence and in the life of all things and beings we see these two forces working unceasingly, each being for the other, and in the experience of expression and response lies the joy of both, in other words, the satisfaction of the Consciousness. The sun expresses, the moon responds; the voice expresses, the ear responds. All the dual aspect in life, such as male and female, shows these two aspects. There is not a single thought, speech, action or event that takes place without the activity of these two, all happiness and success being in their harmony and every fall and failure in its lack. The birth of every thing and being is caused by the meeting of their glance, and death and destruction is the result of their conflict, when either merges into the other and both lose their power.

There are two different ways in which creation takes place from the highest to the lowest plane, intention and accident. The former shows the wisdom of the Creator, which creates all things suited to their purpose, and accident is that which shows in things and beings loss of purpose. All the opposites, such as good and evil, sin and virtue, right and wrong, beauty and ugliness, are accounted for by the above two tendencies of the Creator that work throughout the creation.

The whole creation acts under the law of attraction and repulsion, the former being the affinity which collects and groups atoms and vibrations and all things and beings, this being power and repulsion the lack of it. It is these two that uphold the universe; if one of them were to cease to exist the whole universe would crumble to pieces.

The life of the universe in all its workings is entirely dependent upon the law of tone and rhythm.

The pure Consciousness has, so to speak, limited itself more and more by degrees by entering into the external vehicles, such as the mind and the body, in order to be conscious of something, for the joy of every thing is experienced when it is essayed.

The first state of manifestation of the Consciousness is of a collective nature, in other words a universal spirit, not individual. There is a saying of a Dervish, "God slept in the mineral kingdom, dreamed in the vegetable kingdom, awakened in the animal kingdom, and realized Himself in the human race." Therefore the ultimate aim of the Eternal Consciousness in undertaking a journey to the plane of mortality is to realize its eternal being.

Each of the said kingdoms has sprung from the preceding one and each preceding kingdom has developed into the succeeding kingdom. In the mineral kingdom one sees by a careful study how the rock has developed into metal, and from metal into softer earthy substance, until it develops into the plant. And one sees how the development of the plant creates germs and worms, which we call lives, and how from their germ and worm state of being they develop into insects, birds and beasts. This all shows that nature is working continually to rise to a greater consciousness of life, and finds its satisfaction at last when it has accomplished its journey by rising and has risen to its natural and normal state of being, which it accomplishes in man.

THE LAW OF HEREDITY.

Heredity has been much thought of among all peoples and in all ages. If we look at the animal kingdom we see that the lion cub is never the offspring of the snake nor are toads hatched from pigeon's eggs, the oak tree will not produce dates nor do roses spring from thistles. We see in the East that of all breeds of horses the Arab horse is the best. One slight touch of the whip will make it leap any obstacle, cover any distance, while there are other horses that are like donkeys, on whose backs dozens of lashes are laid and they put one foot forward and stop, and again twenty lashes are given to them and they take one step forward. The Arabs value their horses so highly that they reserve the breed and never allow it to be mixed with any other strain. Among dogs there are some who will follow anyone. Whoever gives them a bone is their master, and if another person gives them meat, they leave the first and run after the other. And there are others who follow only one master, who obey only one and sometimes even sacrifice their life for him.   It depends upon the breed, the heredity.

In the East they have considered this subject of heredity very much and have given great importance to it. We have always seen that the son of a poet will be a poet, the son of a musician is expected to be a musician.   If a man handles weapons they ask him, " Are you the son of a soldier ?" The son of a miner will never do the work of a shepherd, and the son of a shepherd will never do the work of a miner. A great many of the words of abuse have more to do with the parents than with the person to whom they are addressed, and a great many words of praise have to do with the ancestors, not with the person of whom they are spoken. In India we have a family of poets who have been poets for ten or fifteen generations. They are in Rajputana, and are all of them great, wonderful poets. They are called Shighrakavi, improvisors, and are appointed in the courts of the Maharajahs. Their work is to stand up upon any occasion in the assembly and, seeing the occasion and the people present, to recite verses, in rhyme and metre, in the manner suited to the occasion. In ancient times, when often sons of kings and great people were driven from their country and wandered unknown in other lands, the way of recognizing them was always by some test of their quality. It has happened in the history of the world that slaves have become kings, and yet they could not keep themselves from showing from the throne, through their grandeur, glimpses of their slavish nature.

You may ask whether it is the soul that transmits its qualities, or the mind that transmits its qualities, or the body? This is a vast subject. Before explaining it I will say, as to the word soul, that there are some people who call soul those qualities that compose the individuality. This is not the soul but the mind. The soul has no qualities, it is the pure consciousness and therefore it does not transmit any.

When the soul first starts from its original point, it comes first to the world of the Fereshta, the angels, and is impressed with the angelic qualities. The angels are absorbed in the hunger for beauty and the thirst for song. They do not distinguish good and bad, high and low. The infant, who represents the angel on earth, always turns to what appears to it radiant and beautiful. There are two sorts of angels, those who have never manifested as man, and those spirits who upon their way back to the Infinite have reached the world of the angels. Love, light and lyric are the attributes of the latter, from them the soul receives these impressions. Devotion, service and worship are the attributes of the former. The angels are masculine and feminine; the former are called Malak, the latter Hur.

In the world of the angels the soul for years and years enjoys these experiences. When the desire for more experience urges it on, it goes forth and comes to the world of Jinns, which is the astral plane. In the Bible we read that Adam was driven out of Paradise; this means that the wish for more experience makes the soul leave the world of the angels and go to the astral plane and the physical plane.

The occupation of the Jinns is to imagine, reason and think. The Jinns are of two sorts: there are those who have never manifested physically and there are those spirits who have left the earth with all the load of their actions and experiences upon them. The Jinns also are masculine and feminine, and are called Gulman and Peri.

The soul, on its journey from the unseen to the seen world, receives impressions from the souls which are on their return journey from the seen to the unseen. In this way the soul collects the first merits and qualities. It is this which forms a line for the soul to follow, and it is this line that leads it to the parents from whom it inherits its later attributes. The soul receives the impressions of another soul if it is attuned to that other soul. For instance, a soul meeting the soul of Beethoven receives the impression of Beethoven's music, and then is born with the musical qualities of Beethoven. The upholders of the theory of reincarnation say, "He is the reincarnation of Beethoven." The Sufi says that if it is meant that Beethoven's mind is reincarnated in him, it may be said; but because the spirit is from the Unlimited, he says it need not necessarily be called reincarnation. Therefore a person of poetical gifts may be born in the family of a statesman where there never before was a poet.

Each soul is like a ray of the sun or of any light. Its work is to project itself, to go forth as far as it can. It is creative and responsive. It creates its means, its expression, and it is impressed by whatever comes before it, in proportion to its interest in that. The soul goes always to what appears to it beautiful and radiant, and so it goes on and on and finds different qualities and different experiences and collects them round it, until at last it finds the mother's womb.

A child may either not inherit the qualities and defects of its parents or it may inherit them. If the impressions previously received by the soul are stronger it does not inherit them. Very wicked parents may have a very saintly child, and very good parents may have a very bad child.

The mental attributes of the parents are inherited by impression on the mental plane. The thought, the feeling of the parents are inherited by the child as a quality. If the father is engaged in thinking, "I should build an orphanage," the child will have a philanthropic disposition. If the father is thinking, "This person is my enemy, I should revenge myself on him," the child will have a vindictive disposition. If the mother admires something very much, if she thinks, "How beautiful these flowers are," the child will have that love of beauty in its nature. Also the qualities and features of the relations and other persons of whom either of the parents thinks most are impressed on the child.

You will ask me, "A child is often like an uncle or an aunt of the father or mother; why is this?" This has two aspects. It may be either that the father or mother has the qualities of this relation, although in them they have not fully developed, and those qualities develop in the child; or that the grandmother or grandfather or other relation has so much attachment for his descendants that his spirit watches and impresses with his qualities the child that is born in that family.

It is true that genius is transmitted by heredity and develops at every step, but it is sometimes found that the child of a very great person happens to be most ordinary, sometimes the child of a most worthy person proves to be most unworthy. This may be explained in the following manner : every manifestation of genius has three stages, Uruj, Kemal and Zaval, ascent, climax and decline. When the genius is in the ascendant it develops more and more in every generation; when it reaches its climax it surpasses all previous manifestations of genius in that family; when it is in the decline it shows gradually or suddenly the lack or loss of genius. It is thus with families, nations and races.

That which is more outward is given in heritage more than what is more inward. A man may not be very like his father in looks or nature, yet he inherits his property; the State will give the property to the son. It is inherited because it is more outward. The qualities of the body are inherited more than those of the mind, because they are more outward.

Every physical atom of the parents becomes radiant and its qualities are imparted to the child. In the case of a father who has liked drink, the child, of course, is born without the tendency for strong drink at the moment, but as it grows and develops, the cells of its body, being the same as those of the father's, may have the same craving for drink. And so it is with all vices; though the parents would never wish to impart them to their children, yet they do so unconsciously by their weakness and neglect.

Man has often so much concern for his posterity that he earns money and amasses it, not spending it for himself, in order that he may leave it to his children. He even gives his life on the battlefield that his children may enjoy the fruits of the victory. But if he only knew how much influence the life that he leads has on his posterity he would think it of more value to keep his life pure and elevated, both in health and mind, in order that his children may inherit the wealth of humanity, which is much more precious than earthly wealth and possessions.

Coming now to the question whether more qualities are inherited from the paternal side or the maternal side, I will say that the qualities inherited from the father are more deep-seated while those inherited from the mother may be more apparent, because the father's inheritance is the substance, the mother's is the mould. The soul has many more attributes of the father because these are the fundamental, original attributes; the attributes of the mother are added to these, they are more active because they are later attributes. Those qualities which are first impressed upon the soul are stronger and those attributes which are acquired later are more active. From association with its mother, from her training a child acquired very many of her attributes. A man may not like the qualities of his father and may hide them. A small child may have a face just like his mother's, but at some period of his life he will grow so like his father in looks that it is astonishing. A coward by association with brave people may become brave; he may go to the war, but then, when he hears the guns, the cowardice which was the original attribute of his soul will show itself. A child may be very like its mother in appearance, yet the quality is the father's. For instance, if the father is very generous, and the mother is finer, the child will, perhaps, be generous and finer. In this way the evolution of the world goes on by the intermingling of nations and races. Those families who keep themselves segregated in the end become weak and very stupid. For this reason the Prophet in Islam allowed all races and castes to intermarry, because the time had come for the human race to evolve in this way.

You will say, "Then, if we inherit the attributes of our father, our mother, our grandfather and forefathers, and acquire the attributes of the Jinns and angels, how can we help how our character is?" A man may say, "I have a quick temper because my father had a quick temper, I have a changeable disposition because that is in my family; I cannot help this, it is my character." This is true in part, but it is developed by belief in it. The soul acquires and casts off attributes and qualities throughout life. A coward who joins the army by hearing always of bravery, by living with soldiers, may in time feel inclined to go to the war and to fight. A joyous person from being in the society of serious people may become serious, and a sad person from being with cheerful people may become cheerful. The soul acquires only those qualities in which it is interested, it will never take on those in which it is not interested. And the soul keeps only those attributes in which it is interested, it loses those in which it is not interested. However wicked a person may be, however many undesirable attributes he may have inherited, he can throw them all off by the power of will if he does not like them.

You will say, " But can we change our physi-

cal body, can we change our face?" We can.
People become like those of whom they think
strongly or with whom they associate. I have
seen herdsmen, who live with the cattle and sheep,
and from association with the cattle and sheep
their faces had become very like the animals'.
It is our thoughts and feelings that change our
appearance, and if we had control over them we
should develop that appearance that we wish to
develop.

But for those who are walking in the path of
Truth there is no heredity. By realizing their
divine origin they free themselves from all earthly
inheritance. As Christ said " My Father in Heaven," so they realize their origin from the spirit,
and by their concentration and meditation they can
create all the merits they wish for and clear away
from their soul all influences which they do not like
to possess.

REINCARNATION.

When we study religions, comparing them, we
find that part of the world has believed in reincarnation, but most of the world has not held this
belief. Krishna, Shiva and Buddha are said to

have taught the doctrine of reincarnation; Moses, Christ and Muhammed have said nothing about it. This divides religions into two groups.

But when we make a deeper study we see that we can combine the two, for the tendency of the Sufi is rather to unite than to differ.

There are four widely-spread religions, Islam, Christianity, Brahminism and Buddhism, which have great influence upon humanity by their diffusion. Let us ask each what it has to say on the matter.

Islam is silent on this subject, Christianity says nothing. In their scriptures if there may be rarely a verse which supports this idea there will be ten verses which disprove it.

Let us now consider Brahminism. There are four grades of Brahmins, Brahmachari, Grihasta, Vanaprasti, and Sanyassi. The three lower grades will perhaps answer, " Yes, there is reincarnation, but it depends upon our Karma, our actions. If we, who are men, behave like animals, we may come again as animals, we may be a cow, or a dog, or a cat, or else we may be a human being of a lower order than we are now; and if we live a righteous life we shall find ourselves in a better condition in our next incarnation." When we ask the highest authority among Hindus, the Sanyassi, he will say, "You will, perhaps, reincarnate, I shall not. I am Jivan Mukta, free; I am above the cycle of births and deaths."

Let us now see what Buddhism has to say. It says, "The world is in evolution; so we shall by no means become animals, but we evolve into higher and higher incarnations until we have overcome all weaknesses and have reached Nirvana, perfection; then we return no more."

By this we see that there are only two believers in reincarnation, and even these two have contrary beliefs.

We read in the Bible (St. John xiv. 3), "I come again and will receive you unto myself," and (Acts i. 11), ". . . This Jesus which was received up from you into Heaven, shall so come in like manner as ye beheld him going into heaven." This does not refer to the person of Christ, but to the innermost being of the Master, which was in reality the Being of God. If it concerned his person he would have said, "I shall come, but you also will come again, either in a better condition or in a worse state of being," but nothing of the kind is said. One might say, "Why then did the Master say 'I,' why did he not clearly say 'God'?" The answer is that divine personality is the losing of the thought of one's limited self, the absolute merging into the divine and only personality; then the ego becomes the divine ego, the " I " is not identification with the limited personality but with the personality of God. When Christ said " I " he meant God.

One reads the same in the Masnavi of Jelal-ud-Din Rumi, " Seventy-two forms I have worn and have come to witness this same spring of continual change." This also refers to the divine Consciousness which wears various forms and comes to witness this world of changes; it is not the seventy-two times coming of Maulana Rumi himself. Seventy-two is symbolical of many. Otherwise it would mean that since the human creation he visited the earth only seventy-two times, which would be very few times for such a great length of time.

There are many statements in the Koran such as these : " We will change their faces," said of the wicked, and " We will make them monkeys." The real meaning of the former is " We will cause the brightness, or the happiness, of their expression to fade away by throwing light upon their hidden crimes which so long have kept them bright and happy"; it certainly does not mean " We will make a Frenchman a Chinese." The meaning of the latter is " They have imitated that which they were not." "They will be monkeys" means that they will be taken for that which they are in reality and not for that which they falsely pretended to be, in other words, "We will lay bare the mockery of the impostors."

In the Gospel we read (St. John ix. 1-3), ". . . as . . . Jesus . . . passed by he saw a man blind from his birth. And his disciples asked him, saying, Rabbi, did this man sin, or his parents, that he should be born blind? Jesus answered, Neither did this man sin, nor his parents; but that the works of God should be made manifest in him." This needs no interpretation, for it plainly says that the man's blindness was not the punishment of his former sins.

In the Koran it is written, "All are from God and return to Him." This denies a return to earth. Mention is made, however, of another life in the Surah, "Every soul must taste of death, and ye shall only be paid your reward in full on the resurrection day." Here the resurrection is spoken of, the making alive of the souls without the physical body, and it is plainly said that this existence will be as clear and distinct as is our life on earth.

As the world advances in intellectual development it becomes more and more interested in novelty; whatever is new is taken up and often the new idea is accepted and followed. The idea of reincarnation has made a great impression in the present age, because it appeals at once to the scientific faculty and reasoning natures and it also satisfies those who wish to keep a fast hold on their individuality.

I remember, when in my early age I first knew of death, how for hours I became sad, thinking, "This, my body, the only means of experiencing life, will be one day in the grave. I shall be away from all things and beings that are the interest of life to me to-day. This whole environment which interests me and keeps me engaged all day long will be one day a mist; neither shall I see anybody nor will anybody see me; all whom I love to-day will be one day separated from me." Now my own experience in the past clearly tells me how others must feel at the idea of turning into what seems nothing after being something. It is just as it is when a dream interests us so much that if we wake up in the midst of it and realize at once that we were dreaming, we yet like to close our eyes and give ourselves up to the enjoyment of the experience. Such is the case of all those who are so much interested in the dream of life that the idea of death, which is a more real state of being, is horrible to them. They would rather live a life unreal but individual than a life real but unrealized.

The idea of reincarnation often comforts those who think that it is too soon to renounce the pleasures of life in order to commune with God. " Perhaps," they say, " in our next life on earth we shall achieve what we have not achieved in this." Also it consoles those who have lost their loved ones, for they think these are not lost for ever, but will be born again, and often they look for them whenever a child is born among their acquaintance. It consoles those people also who have not obtained the fruit of their desires in this life and have always longed and hoped for something which could not be gained; these build their only hope on gaining the same in their next incarnation.

This idea often becomes a great hindrance to the real spiritual attainment, though it is helpful to a person who is discontented with his life, suffering from pain, poverty or illness and thinks that it is his Karma to suffer this and that, then, when he has paid the uttermost farthing, his days will change. Then he has no more complaint to make; though he knows he has not committed in this life such sins as to be punished so, still he thinks that there is justice, as he has perhaps sinned in his past life. The idea seems reasonable, especially to a person who looks at life from a practical point of view. " Every man weighs the world on his own scales." And the thought of reincarnation is still more helpful to those who do not believe in God or know His being, also to those who neither believe in everlasting life nor can understand it. For some people it is very consoling to think that they will come on this earthly plane again and again, brought there by their Karma, rather than to think, as many materialists do, "When we are dead we are done with for ever."

The reason why the doctrine of reincarnation was taught to the Hindus and Buddhists must have been that the people of India at that time were very much developed intellectually, in philosophy, in science, in logic, in the material phenomena, and believed in law more than in love.

In the present age, especially in the West, people are beginning now to search for truth by the light of science and logic, as did the Hindus of the Vedic period. The peoples of India were working along the same lines at the origin of Brahminism and still more in the time of Buddhism.

Then, especially among the Mongolians, the people most advanced in arts and sciences, the enlightened were very logical and scientific, with little devotional tendency, and the masses had innumerable objects of worship. There the average person could not conceive the idea of the soul, the hereafter and God as it was propagated in another part of the East by the Hebrew prophets, so the theory of reincarnation was the best means of appealing to their reason instantly in order to break their former ideas. But as it is the nature of the human heart to worship someone, naturally their worship was directed to Buddha.

There is every probability that this idea came originally from the Devata, the divine messengers born among Hindus. Each of these declared that he was the incarnation of Brahma, God, and each in turn claimed to be the reincarnation of the preceding Deva, whom he succeeded. In claiming to be the incarnation of Brahma or the Deva they succeeded they did not mean that in their guise God was born or their predecessor reborn but that they had realized God or that they possessed the same knowledge and mission as their predecessor. When the others asked them, "Of what are we the incarnations?" they were obliged to give them some explanation of a like kind, and they told each one that which his condition of life suggested to them.

When the four Varnas, castes, were made in

India, Brahmin, Kshattria, Vayesha and Kshruddra, these were not in fact different castes but classes. The whole administration was arranged in this way : Brahmins to study, meditate and be worshipped, Kshattrias to fight and guard the country, Vayeshas to carry on commerce, and Kshuddras to labour and serve. None save Brahmins had Adhicar, the right to study the Vedas, the books of mysticism and philosophy; even Kshattrias and Vayeshas had to be content in the worship of the Brahmins and with the Purana, the religion taught in legends; Kshuddras, the labouring class, were denied even that.

It has always been the tendency of the stronger and more intelligent men to keep the weak and simple down. Owing to the inclination of the higher caste to keep itself pure from further admixture of the lower classes, a religious rule was made enforcing the belief that the Kshuddra, the lowest, could not become a Vayesha, the Vayesha could not become a Kshattria, nor a Kshattria be admitted among Brahmins, the highest and supreme class of the time, unless by his good actions he had made it possible that he should be born, in the next incarnation, in a family of the higher caste. The idea of reincarnation, as a belief generally held, was made the basis of the Hindu religion, upon which the whole building of Brahminism was erected. But everyone in the world has an inclination to raise his head and climb up higher, if he can, from that level upon which he may have been set in life. Verily the light of truth, the beauty of nature, the desire for freedom, the idea of unity cannot be covered, sooner or later it flashes forth.

The law of Karma, action, is the philosophy which a reasoning brain holds in support of re-incarnation, saying "There is no such being as God as an intervener in our life's affairs, but it is we who by our actions produce results similar to them. There is the ever-ruling law of cause and effect, therefore every occurrence in life must be in accordance with it. If we do not get the results of our good or wicked deeds immediately that is because they need time to mature so as to produce similar results; if they do not in this life, then the law drags us to be born again in another incarnation, in order to experience in that the effect of our deeds."

Looking at the wheel of evolution one sees that we do not always rise, we also fall, we do not always become better people, sometimes man grows worse than he was. The nature of evolution is like a wheel turning round, not rising always. This gives us reason to doubt how far

the Buddhistic idea of better and better reincar-
nations can prove to be logical.

In support of reincarnation a story is told of
two friends who were going out for a holiday.
One said, " Let us go to the temple, there we shall
hear the name of God, we shall be uplifted."
The other said, " You are always such a melan-
choly boy; you always find such dull occupations.
We will not go to the temple, we will go where
we can enjoy ourselves; we will go to the Gaiety."
The first said, " I do not like that idea, I will not
go with you." So they parted. The one who
went to the temple on his way met with an accident
from a waggon in the road and his foot was
crushed. He thought, " What a good thing that
my friend did not come with me; he too would
have been injured." The other on his way to the
Gaiety had great luck, he found a purse full of
gold coins. He thought, " Thank God! If my
friend had been with me, I should have had to
share this with him." As soon as the first had
recovered a little, he went to a Brahmin and asked
him, " What was the reason that I, who was on
my way to the temple, had the bad luck to have
my foot crushed, and my friend, who was on his
way to the Gaiety, had the good luck that he
found this gold purse?" The Brahmin said,

"The reason is that you in your former life did some very bad action, and you were meant to be killed, and not only killed but hanged for everybody to see, but it happened that only your foot was crushed. Your friend in his former life did some very good action and he was meant to be a king, but it happened for his present sins that he only found a purse full of gold coins."

If we believe in the idea we must first understand where evil ends and where good begins. It has never been possible for a deep thinker to draw a line between good and evil. What distinction do we find, from this point of view, between good and evil, if it be seen with a magnifying view? None but the difference of degree and difference of view. What seems good to one person to the other does not, and so it is with evil. Also every evil to the eye of the seer is a lesser good, which in comparison with the greater good appears different from that and so is called evil.

And if the wheel of births and deaths depends upon cause and effect, I should say it must go on for ever and ever and there would never be an end to it. According to this doctrine not only the punishment of our sins, but even the reward of the good we have done would drag us back to earth; we shall have to come back on earth in any case. Even should we not wish for a reward we cannot stop the wheel, for we have no power over nature's law. What a helpless condition! Neither does God intervene in our affairs, that He might stop it with His all-might, nor can we, helpless human beings subject to the law of cause and effect.

Again considering this subject we see that everything existing can be destroyed by some other thing or substance. There is no stain that cannot be cleaned off by some chemical solution. There is no record which cannot be erased from the surface of the paper, even if it is engraved upon stone it can be scraped off. Man, the master of the whole creation, has found the means to destroy all things, and it is very astonishing if he is unable to find a solution to wipe off the impressions of Karma, life's deeds, so as to escape the wheel of births and deaths, when he professes to know all things of the earth and claims to have solved all the mysteries of the heavens.

Some believers in God say in support of re-incarnation, " God is just. There are many who are lame or blind or unhappy in life, and this is the punishment for the faults they have committed before, in a former incarnation. If it were not so, that would be injustice on the part of God." That makes God only a reckoner and not a lover, and it restricts Him to His justice like a judge bound by the law. The judge is the slave of law, the forgiver is its master. In fact we ourselves, limited as we are, have mercy in us, so that often if someone has done something against us we would forgive. If he only bows before us we say, " He has humiliated himself, I will forget." I have seen mothers who, even if their son has caused them much sorrow, if, when he has any trouble, he only says, " Mother, I have done this, but you are the one to whom I can come for sympathy," will say, " My child, I forgive you, though at the time it made me sad." If we, who are full of faults and errors, having in us that little spark of mercy inherited from God, can forgive, how can we think that God, the most Merciful, will reckon our faults like a judge ? We are as little children before Him.

Regarding God as a personal being, how can we think that He, Whose being is love, Whose action is love, Who is all love, can weigh our actions as a judge would ?

A judge, also, when someone is brought before him, after he has looked into the case, says, " I have looked into your case and I find that you are guilty. You are given six months', or five years', or ten years' imprisonment. Your fault is very

bad and so you must learn not to do it again."
But if we go to the blind and lame and ask them,
"Were you given this in punishment? Were
you told so?" they say, "No, we were told
nothing." Now how are we to imagine that God
could be so unjust as to punish them and yet not
tell them of their crime?

If we return, then every child that is born
should know what he was before. If only excep-
tional ones feel that they know what they were
before, in another life, then it may be a delusion,
a pretence, or a scheme for gaining notoriety by
appearing to know what everybody does not
know.

If God is most merciful how could He govern
us only by law void of love and compassion, when
even we human beings forget and forgive another's
fault in spite of law, reason and logic, when
moved by love, our divine inheritance? "God
is love," not law. Love in its lower manifestation
turns into law by forming habits, yet it is not law
which rules love, it is love that controls law.

The idea of forgiveness is the result of our
idealizing God. As we idealize God so He proves
to be. Sometimes the sins of a whole life may be
wiped off in one instant; sometimes all the virtue
and piety of a whole life may be lost by one sin.

A story is told that Moses was going to Mount Sinai and on his way he met a very pious person, who said to him, "Moses, speak to God of me. All my life I have been pious, I have been virtuous, I have prayed to God, and I have had nothing but troubles and misfortunes." A little later Moses met a man sitting in the street with a bottle of liquor. He called out, "Moses! Where are you going?" Moses said, "To Mount Sinai." The man called out, "To Mount Sinai? Then speak to God of me," for he was drunk.

Moses went to Mount Sinai and he told God of the pious person whom he had met. God said, "For him there is a place in the Heavens." Then he told God of the drunken man whom he had met. God said, "He shall be sent to the worst possible place in Hell."

Moses went away and first he met the drunken man. He told him, "God says you shall be sent to the worst possible place in Hell." The man said, "God spoke of me?" and he was so overjoyed that he could not contain himself but began to dance, just as a poor man might be overjoyed if he heard that a king had spoken of him, even if the king had said nothing good of him. Then he said, "How happy should I be that He, the Creator and Sovereign of the universe, knows me, the great sinner." Then Moses told the pious person what God had said. He said, " Why not? I have spent all my life in the worship of God and in piety, sacrificing all else in life; and therefore I am entitled to have it."

Both the pious person and the drunkard died, and Moses was curious to know what had become of them. He went to Mount Sinai and asked God. God said, "The pious person is in Hell, and the drunken man is in Heaven." Moses thought, "Does God break His word?" God said, "The drunkard's joy on hearing that We had spoken of him has wiped out all his sins. The pious person's virtue was worthless. Why could he not be satisfied if We made the sun shine and sent the rain?"

If anyone were to weigh his righteous actions against the myriad favours of God, all the righteous actions of every moment of his life would not compare with one moment of God's favour. Therefore the devotee forgets his righteous actions, looking only at the favour of God. " When the pious was looking for the beloved God among the righteous, His mercy cried out, ' Come hither. I am busy among sinners, forgiving them their sins.' " Amir.

MAN, THE SEED OF GOD.

Man may most justly be called the seed of God. God the Infinite, most conscious within Himself, embraces His nature full of variety; in this way He is one and He is all. The whole manifestation is just like a tree sprung from the divine root. Nature is like its stem and all the aspects of nature are like the branches, the leaves, the fruit, and the flower, and from this tree again the same seed is produced, the human soul, which was the first cause of the tree. This seed is the spirit of man, and as God comprehends the whole universe within Himself, being one, so man contains within himself the whole universe as His miniature. "In our own image we have created man." Koran. Therefore neither can God be anything else than what He is, for the very reason that He is one and at the same time He is all, nor can man; neither can man be reincarnated nor can God.

The men of science of to-day have admitted the fact that all the skin of man is changed in so many years and they have been able to discover that each atom of man's constitution changes so many times in life, renewing his body each time. If the body is subject to change, so is the mind, and it is only by these that man's person is identified. Again, in our food and drink we live upon so many small lives and so many small lives live upon us, dwelling in our blood, veins, tubes, and in the skin, all of which constitutes our individuality. And in the mind our every thought and feeling is as alive as we, even such beings as the elementals, demons and angels, which are created within us, from us, and of us, and yet may as fitly be called individuals as we. So in the end of the examination it is hard for a man to find whether he exists as one or many.

In our dreams all the inhabitants of our mind resurrect, forming a world within ourselves. We see in the dream things and beings, a friend, a foe, an animal, a bird, and they come from nowhere, but are created out of our own selves. This shows that the mind of an individual constitutes a world in itself, which is created and destroyed by the conscious or unconscious action of the will, which has two aspects, intention and accident. We have experience of this world of mind even while awake, but the contrast between the world within and without makes the world without concrete and the world within inconcrete.

Someone may ask, " If all that we see in the dream are we ourselves then why do we even in the dream see ourselves as an entity separate from all other things before us in the dream?"

The answer is, " Because the soul is deluded by our external form, and this picture it recognizes as I, and all other images and forms manifesting before it in the dream stand in contrast to this I; therefore the soul recognizes them as other than I."

Therefore, if it is one individual that reincarnates, should we hold our changeable body to be an individual or our mind, both of which appear to be one and at the same time many? One might ask Jack, " Which part of yourself is Jack, the eye, the nose, the ear, or the hand or foot, which each of them have a particular name? Or are your thoughts and feelings Jack? They are numerous, changeable, and diverse; you name them as such an imagination, such a feeling." This shows that Jack stands aloof as the owner of all the finer and grosser properties that have grouped and formed an illusion before him, which, reflected upon his soul, makes him say, " I, Jack." He is the owner of all that he realizes around and about him, and yet each atom and vibration which has composed his illusionary self is liable to change, to a separate and individual birth and death.

The soul on its journey to the Infinite cannot turn back halfway; and when it reaches that goal, it experiences only the light, the wisdom, the love of God, and it loses two things: it loses all the marks of the experiences and thoughts of its manifestation and it gradually loses its individuality and merges in the infinite, divine Consciousness.

If an earthen thing is thrown into the water it has a tendency to go to the bottom, to its own element. If water is accompanying fire on its journey its water part still drips down as steam. When fire travels with the air it takes its smoke so far, but in its higher spheres it gets rid of the fire. When ether turns into spirit it drops its contact with the air element. Thus it is with the soul; on its return journey it gives back all the above properties to their own sources, thus lightening its load on its way towards its own element. The earthly body goes to earth, its water part to the world of waters, its heat to the kingdom of heat, its air to the spheres of the air, its ether into the ethereal regions. Its impressions, thoughts, feelings, merits, qualities go as far as they can reach, and remain at their stations, wherever they are meant to be. Then it is the soul in its own essence that is left, merging into the ocean of Consciousness where nothing of its previous property remains.

Our personality is just like a bubble in the

water.   As little probability as there is of a bubble once merged in the sea coming out again composed of the same portion of water so little probability is there for the soul once merged in the ocean of Consciousness to come out again formed of the self-same portion of Consciousness. The bubble may come back in the same place with the same portion of water, or it may be another portion of water.   There may be half of the first drop of water in the second bubble, there may be a small part, or there may be some portion of water added to it.

If one bubble comes, and we call that bubble John and then we call another Jacob and a third Henry, yet they are all the same water, and if we call the water John they are all the same John. All is the same spirit, the same Life, involving itself into all the forms and the names. From this point of view there is no I, no you, no he, no she, no it, in the light of reality; all are but the differences of a moment.

Every bubble loses both reflections or any properties it possessed during its existence as soon as it merges in the water, and if once in a thousand chances it should come formed of the self-same portion of water, it would not retain its previous property.   In the same way supposing, as a mere assumption, that the self-same portion of Consciousness, which, in the first place, is not so substantial and stable as water, could possibly appear again on the surface without any addition or deduction, it is utterly impossible that it should still possess its past qualities and impressions, for it has been absolutely purified by sinking into the Consciousness. And if even a drop of ink loses its ink property in the sea, why should not the ocean of Consciousness purify its own element from all elements foreign to itself?

As Hinduism teaches the doctrine that bathing once in the Sangum at the confluence of the two rivers can purify man from all life's sins, how can it deny that this bath of the soul, sinking into the Consciousness even once, purifies the soul from all the properties it has gathered during its previous life? In the first place, the nature itself of absorption in the Spirit is purification from the material state of being, and the very nature of manifestation is for the soul to come new and fresh.

Suppose we grant that cream is the reincarnation of milk and butter is the third step of the reincarnation of milk and its fourth reincarnation may be called ghee; then the question arises, of what is milk the reincarnation? Milk is composed of several chemical substances, and its chemical arrangement changes the name, savour, smell, and effect. Butter cannot be called milk, nor is ghee cream. If there is anything which seems to be existing through all the manifestation of the milk, it is the inner ruling current which groups and scatters atoms, compelling them to change, which may be likened to the soul.

Also, if Jack has reincarnated as John, or John has reincarnated as Jack, what were both in the beginning? Were they two or one? If one became two, then one could become thousands, millions, and still he is one only.

The shooting forth of the soul from the Consciousness can be symbolized as an arrow. The arrow shot up in the air goes up as far as the will and power of the sender has destined it to go, and when it reaches its utmost height its return begins. The death of the physical being is the return of that arrow. Of course, on its return it may be detained on its way, perhaps, as the arrow is sometimes caught in the branches of a tree, but it returns some day or other to the earth, its own element. It does not go up again from there by any means. So it is with the human soul, which, after finishing its course on earth, returns to its origin, drawn by its power of attraction.

When we look at the world we see that everything makes a circle. The plant grows from the seed to its developed state and returns to dust. Man grows from childhood to youth, to maturity, then to old age. This, it is said, is an argument for our passing through many lives. But it is not the circle which journeys, but the point which, journeying, forms the circle and returns to the place from which it started. It is the Consciousness that performs the journey and not the individual soul.

The drops of water in a fountain go up, some higher, some lower, some go a very little way, some rise very high. When each drop falls down it sinks into the stream, flowing away with it and does not rise again, although the water of the same stream rises again and falls again in drops, which proves to us the fact that the water rises and falls continually, not the drop; yet apparently it rises and falls as drops, though the portion of water in every drop is different.

One point which the reincarnationists hold in support of their doctrine is the traces of unusual genius or gift found in a child who does not seem to inherit the same from his ancestors and cannot acquire it from his surroundings. Sometimes in the slums a child is born which has great poetical genius which could not be found in its father or mother nor in its forefathers, or a great musical gift which could not be found in its father or grandfather or ancestors.

The soul before its coming on the face of the earth for a very, very long time, on its way to manifestation, gathers the impressions of those souls whom it meets on its way and takes on their attributes. In this way the attributes of the past ones are manifested again. A soul may receive the impressions of one soul or of a few souls or of many souls.

The soul on its way toward manifestation may meet the soul of a genius in poetry or music and take with it these impressions. When some very great or very good or philanthropic person has died you will find that soon after a child of like qualities will be born to balance the world. A child may be born with the qualities of Alexander the Great. This is because the new soul coming out towards manifestation has met the soul of Alexander and has become impressed with all his qualities or part of his qualities. Such a one may assert "I am the reincarnation of Alexander." But the soul of Alexander does not return. If it did, then every soul that has left this life would know of his former lives.

Much of the difference of understanding is the

difference of words. If someone says that the soul is the world of impressions which the Consciousness holds before it and the spirit is the Consciousness, then he may say that the soul returns.

When the child of unpoetical ,parents sings, making up words of its own, this shows that it has received the impression of some poetical soul. The soul that comes to the surface is more responsive than creative; it is not creative, because it has nothing to give. The soul on its return is creative; it imparts its experiences there. For example, an unused photographic plate takes the impression of the object before it, but the used plate reflects its impression on to the paper. Suppose, for instance, the soul of Vishnu meets a soul on its way to manifestation, this powerful soul may impress the other with its attributes. Then that soul may say, "I am Krishna, the reincarnation of Vishnu." The soul is impressed with whatever comes before it. Sometimes children of quite ordinary parents may be so impressed by a great person in whose presence they are that they themselves become great. And as man's personality is nothing but an agglomeration of his thoughts and impressions, the inheritor of that may be called the reincarnation of the past one, although his soul is his own.

Sometimes a child appears to see and understand very much of what is going on around him from his infancy. Sometimes a young man sees and understands more than an old person. Such people are supposed by the average person to be old souls, and the reincarnationists take it as a proof of the doctrine of reincarnation. But, really speaking, knowing and understanding do not depend upon learning; knowledge is the soul's quality. The knowledge of the spirit has been man's in all ages. An old person does not need to read many books in order to learn that he was once a little child; he knows it, it is his past experience. So the soul knows its own experience; it needs only a little awakening to make it self-conscious.

When the Shah of Persia wished to have the history of Persia written by some literary person there was no one found who could do it until the mystic poet Firdausi said that he would write it. And he wrote, from his inner knowledge, the *Shah-Namah,* the history of the Shahs of Persia. If he had this knowledge from the recollection of his own previous lives he must have reincarnated repeatedly in Persia and in Persia only, uninterruptedly, endowed each time with the same degree of intelligence, so as to acquire and retain all this knowledge.

There is nothing which the soul cannot know, for the whole objective existence is made by the soul for its own **use,** and therefore it is not astonishing if man possesses great qualities that he has not inherited, and if he has knowledge of all things through revelation, not by learning. It is astonishing only when he lacks this, and that is owing to the globes upon globes of the objective world covering the light of the soul.

CONCLUSION.

I first believed without any hesitation in the existence of the soul, and then I wondered about the secret of its nature. I persevered and strove in search of the soul, and found at last that I myself was the cover over my soul. I realized that that which believed in me, and that which wondered in me, that which persevered in me, and that which found in me, and that which was found at last was no other than my soul. I thanked the darkness that brought me to the light, and I valued the veil which prepared for me the vision in which I saw myself reflected, the vision produced in the mirror of my soul. Since then I have seen all souls as my soul and realized my soul as the soul of All, and what bewilderment it was

when I realized that I alone was, if there were anyone, and I am whatever and whoever exists, and
I shall be whoever there will be in the future, and
there was no end to my happiness and joy.
Verily, I am the seed and I am the root and I am
the fruit of this tree of life.

CPSIA information can be obtained
at www.ICGtesting.com
Printed in the USA
BVHW050016230620
582039BV00011B/775